Wistful Winter

Serena Joy Laverty

BookLeaf
Publishing

India | USA | UK

Presentation by *BookLeaf Publishing*

Web: www.bookleafpub.com

E-mail: info@bookleafpub.com

ISBN: 978-93-5744-367-8

First edition 2022

*For all those who said I could when I no longer
thought I had it in me.*

PREFACE

What if the what-ifs we whisper at night
Are the what-ifs of us all,
Breathing a collective sigh?

This line randomly landed on my tongue one late-November night when I was preparing to embark on the 21-day writing challenge that would become this book. Sometimes inspiration feels impossibly out of sight, and you find yourself searching for it in the nooks and crannies of your mind as you stare at a blank page. Other times, it whacks you over the head unexpectedly, and you have to abruptly stop what you are doing to jot your idea down before it disappears. The line I have shared here is an example of the latter experience. It popped into my mind as if another voice spoke it, and I typed it down onto my computer before I could even question what it was I was writing.

The idea that all of humanity is connected – from past to present to whatever future lies ahead – has always intrigued me. As a child, I used to stare at the people in the cars passing by and wonder about their life stories, marvelling at the fact that for just a brief moment in time, our paths had intersected, only never to see each other again. At the grocery store, I would stare at the faces of the shoppers passing by and wonder what had brought them there to this exact moment, with their mannerisms and quirks and need to buy chocolate milk at 5 pm on a Tuesday. I often thought about how those brief interactions with strangers altered our life courses in tiny, minuscule ways that we would never know about or understand, but that was somehow a part of this larger story of life in which we are all connected.

Sometimes, it would frighten me, thinking about how much of an impact I could have on other people's lives. For a long time, I moved through life as an observer on the outskirts, making myself as small as possible so as not to interfere with or harm another person's life. When I was a teenager, I began to recognize this tendency in myself. I wrote in my journal one night: "The amount of impact I can have on a person's life scares me. The fact that somebody could long for me, spend time thinking about me, feel sad or angry or hurt because of me, scares me. So I tread as lightly as I can and keep to myself. I am so afraid of how my life intertwines with others. I am so afraid of making mistakes. I am afraid."

It probably is not shocking to you that this "treading lightly" strategy did not lead me to great places. I did not realize that depression, anxiety, and low self-esteem were at play, causing me to believe that I was somehow unworthy of genuine connection as I might dampen someone else's light. The more I withdrew from the people around me, the worse my mental health became. And, as it turned out, remaining passively uninvolved on the sidelines - hiding my emotions and appreciation for those around me out of fear of rejection - led to me hurting a lot of people, which was precisely what I had hoped to avoid. I soon learned that I could not simply extract myself from the people around me and not affect them - I was already inextricably tied to those in my life, and remaining uninvolved was just as consequential as letting someone entirely in. I, just like you, am connected to a larger constellation of human souls, whether I like it or not. My actions or inaction influence those around me, and there is no escaping it.

These days, in the third year of a worldwide pandemic, I think we have paradoxically become more aware of how connected we are whilst simultaneously feeling more isolated than ever. When it comes to the virus, we know that our actions or inaction can influence the health and safety of the next person. And yet, with widespread lockdowns and work-from-home orders, we have become accustomed to living more isolated than ever. With more time and silence to be with our thoughts, I think there is tremendous potential to work through emotions and trauma we have previously not allowed ourselves to confront. At the same time, I believe there is a temptation to continue stifling those pesky feelings and doing whatever we can to manage them independently, rather than reaching out to those around us who may be able to empathize.

Connection – truly genuine, messy, authentic, real connection – can be terrifying to those of us who have spent years in hiding. It is frightening, but it is also all that truly matters; human connection is where life happens. So, come as you are, in your fears and weakness and don't be surprised when you find that everyone else is a mess too. We need each other because we were created as a part of a greater whole. The sighs you release, the longings you whisper, are not isolated no matter how lonely you feel. Somewhere, someone else is longing for something similar too. Somewhere, someone else is sighing in time with you.

This book is sectioned into two parts. Poems one through ten are introspective and emotionally turbulent. In my mind, this first half is the "retreating inwards" part of the book – the part for when you are curled up by a fire watching the winter storm outside and feeling a pang of regret, loneliness, longing. Nothing is sugar-coated here: these poems are inspired by mine or others' experiences of hardship and longing. I believe we must accept, validate, and work through our feelings before real growth can occur. The second half of the book is when you are ready to brave the winter storm; it is about learning to let go of all that is weighing you down and connect back with the world again. This part of the book acknowledges the pain of the first half but provides a more optimistic lens to look through going forward; it is what I call the "reaching out" poems.

Allow this book of poetry to validate your feelings of despair, but also allow it to be a comforting reminder that you are not alone. And when you are ready to step out into the world again, there is a whole community of people just waiting to let you in. There is a whole life out there of connection and hope, and new beginnings. I promise.

~ Serena Joy

Part One:
Retreating Inwards

journey to authenticity

Where do you go to find
the pieces of yourself you left behind –
when you were lost in the chaos and storm
that all but ruined the life you had before?
How much of you *then* exists now?
Did your heart harden over with the darkening
clouds?
Is there still light within you –
just waiting to peak out?
Is it forever hidden
since the day that you found out
that the world is not as kind as it seems –
that its cruelty will come to haunt you
and tear up your dreams?
Or did it vanish when you chose to become
the person *they* wanted
instead of the person you are?

once upon a time

Once upon a time, I met a boy.
He had eyes that burned warm like the sun:
a stare so hot
that I could not bear to look into them
or I risked losing all the breath
within my lungs.
He had eyes that,
when lost in thought,
were so deep a brown
I thought it must be where all
the world's secrets were hidden.
He had eyes that,
when he smiled,
lit up like stars
and danced when they looked at me,
making me feel welcome
and at home.

And he had eyes,
that sometimes,
would greet mine seriously
and just for a moment,
seemed to mirror all the thoughts and emotions
I had ever felt:
to reach into the soul behind my own eyes,
to say hello,

to say they understood me somehow,
to say that somehow they were already a part of
me.

But of course,
I remember the first time his eyes broke
in front of me
and retreated with wounds.
And I remember the first time they finally stared
at me blankly
with all its light gone.
But I do not want to remember those times;
they only serve as reminders
that I threw shade over that warm sun,
that I drew blinds over the window to the earth's
secrets,
that I shut the door on the home that welcomed
me,
that I said goodbye to the soul that said hello to
mine.

Once upon a time, I met a boy.
He had eyes that burned warm like the sun.
But I did not feel worthy of their gaze.
And so I turned to the last page of the story -
where it said "the end" -
before it had ever really begun.

beyond what meets the eye

What fragment of my whole have you chosen to
cling onto?
Have you decided I am meek –
the perfect doormat for your feet?
Or have I voiced my opinions too loud;
did it make you uncomfortable –
me speaking out?
Am I the perfect little daydream you always
hoped I was?
Or am I a perfect disappointment –
now that my flaws have been unveiled?
You claim to understand,
you claim to know my soul,
you claim to have it figured out –
how my story goes.
But you catch a mere glimpse of my reflection –
the one I let you see.
For you, I may smile,
I may even show my teeth,
but you do not know what's hidden
in the deep waters beneath
the tip of the iceberg
you claim to fully see.

winter night

How envious I am
of the way the snowflakes dance -
gracefully descending into a blanket of white
as pale grey skies darken to an indigo night.
On the other side of frosted glass,
hands frozen 'round a steaming cup,
I feel my spirits lifting with the drifting snow
as if I escaped the suffocating hold
that this world's rules and norms
pressed onto my soul.

Alas, I am free
to dance and to laugh,
to embrace my own wild streak,
and the dreams I once had.
Who said I must live by today's solemn rules?
I can be the one who resists
the cookie-cutter mould.
Forget about bills and the need to succeed,
I wish only to live true to myself and spread
peace.

A wind picks up now,
it swirls round and round,
picking up snowflakes and tossing them against
the ground;

it whistles and howls and sneaks through the
door's cracks.
I pull my cup of tea closer,
but it too has grown cold.

Who am I to think I am so special as to avoid
the 9-5 job,
the meaningless void?
What would they think?
How would I survive –
without the security of money
and a title to feed my pride?

The howls mute to a faint hum,
the wind settles down,
snowflakes slow their fall.
I watch in awe
as they swirl and twist;
some land against the windowpane,
some daintily kiss.
They twirl and they leap
in their distinct, fragile shapes;
they taunt me as I stare at their delicate blitz:
Oh, the freedom they have
is the freedom I crave.

longing

Are you willing to let it slip away -
all the what-ifs -
the delicate beginning rush?
Are you willing to pretend you forget
the way the sun danced on my cheek
that morning when we first met:
The way our lives intertwined
so suddenly, so incomprehensibly -
as if the hands of fate had carved out our paths
for that very moment when you called out
and despite all my hesitations,
despite all my fears,
I replied.

It seems you are willing to let it slip away,
to pretend,
to forget.
It seems that I am willing too;
for now, our paths that once crossed
stand a canyon apart -
the distance too wide now
to reach across
a river that has long since dried up.

And yet, I wonder still
about what could have been,

and ever so often, I wonder
if you do too.
For if we only knew each other's thoughts,
maybe we would not be so willing
to let it all slip away
into a distant moment of the past -
into a distant memory.

atonement

Where can I go
to vanish from your view?
Your glow is incandescent -
it lights up the whole room.
I've hid my light for years,
I did not let it shine;
I failed to heed the warning
of the verse from the Divine.

I peer at my reflection
In smudged up broken glass -
the splinters of my face
I cannot recognize at last.
I have fallen from the pedestal
I stood at as a teen;
I no longer hold the virtues
or the halo from their dreams.

For years I sat in darkness -
waiting for your voice;
Then, alas, when sun embraced me
I ran from the looming void.
I gathered up the diamonds
that shone like enticing eyes,
but the sparkle they bore was fleeting -
the high dwindled until it died.

In the bleak skies that came after,
disenchantment, my old friend,
returned to find me weaker
then the moment we first met.
I find myself here now
chasing shadows and moments past -
hoping for an answer,
longing for a way back.

Your warmth feels foreign now
to a soul that has been cold -
your light too hot and blinding
for my eyes to behold.
Do I run,
do I hide,
do I wait for your rage?
Do I stay,
do I reveal,
do I lay at your feet?

And do you remember me
like you said you always would?
Is there still grace for me -
the disillusioned fool?
My calamitous choices
shattered my potential;
are your weathered hands still there
reaching out to break my downfall?

for now

Oh, what I would do
to go back in time
to when the ground beneath our feet was steady–
the future of the Earth assumed –
and the blessed assurance of comforting arms
there to quiet the looming anxiety,
the gut feeling,
that all that we knew was coming to an end.

For now, we hover at the cliff's edge of
a pinnacle moment in history
that perhaps future generations
will tell in awe to their children
of how we somehow made it through.
Or perhaps,
will only be remembered by the stars
when the last tired moan of the Earth
echoes into the universes,
and the dust finally settles in silence.

For now, we stand in the in-between,
uncertain how this story will end:
Will the war we initiated against
ourselves
kill us in the end?
Or will we be the heroes?
Persevering despite all odds,
writing a new ending

to humanity's tragic beginning.

But what if we are too tired?
Numb from the constant barrage
of bad news and heartache
on this nauseating path.
It is far too much to carry
on our shoulders,
on our own.
And I have this sinking feeling
we're beyond
what human hands can mend.

For now, I stand at my windowpane –
lulled by the gentle descent of snow,
embraced by the warm comfort of home,
enveloped in a bubble of privilege –
observing the chaos
from the outside looking in.
I hear their cries of pain,
their cries of sorrow,
their shame,
their bitterness,
their grief.
I watch in disgust at the injustice inflicted
by power-hungry thieves,
and the waste accumulated
by our own willful greed.
I watch in horror at the death and destruction –
sickness spreading like wildfire,
and the colourful burst of wildlife

dissipating to half of what once was.

13

But what can I do?
What can I do
to help heal a wound
as deep as a black hole?
I contemplate from a distance,
from afar,
by the warmth of a fire
on a quiet winter evening,
while war rages beyond.
It will soon reach my doorstep,
of this I am sure:
The chaos I see
is only the calm before the storm.

frost

He did not know
the reason I slipped away
into the shadows,
but I know he felt it
when the moment stopped
and blue frost came
to cause our budding rose
to shrivel up.

I had cut my hands
on the thorny stem -
I bled scarlet red
on the ground -
and I knew it would not stop
if I waited around.
So I withdrew and
watched the rose disappear
beneath frozen ground;
and I hid
as the flurries of white
released like tears
from grey clouds.

It is better this way,
I thought to myself,
I was saving him

from my pain.
But when the blizzard cleared
I saw him bleeding too -
scarlet red
over pure white snow.

elegy for my childhood

I mourn for her -
the wide-eyed,
fragile girl
with a pounding heart
and timid stance,
backed into a corner
and told to stay there.

With watchful,
sensitive
orbs of blue,
she stood on the sidelines
soaking in
their pain and their misery,
their joy and their glory;
she was privy to it all
but never the main character
in the story.

But on the sidelines, she wept
and she shook with fear;
she felt it in her bones
that danger was near.
She turned their pain inwards -
a harsh voice on herself -
she punished her body

and swallowed her tears.

She wasted away
to a thin outer shell;
the light in her dimmed,
she was anything but well.
She did not cry for help,
she did not know how;
she only tried and tried again
to make her inner critic proud.

One day she would collapse
then again,
and again.
She almost thought it was over,
but new light came pouring in
when she learned to lean in
to the love
that was always there,
and a grace that was abundant
and silenced her
fears.

She is older,
stronger now,
and more present
in her own life;
For I learned to love
the child

who once endured
pain and strife.
I hold her in my arms;
I wipe away her tears;
I remind her she is safe now,
and true serenity is near.

a farewell to cynicism

19

They say ignorance is bliss
and I'm miserable as it is;
perhaps a dash of naïveté –
a cup of blind hope –
is what my soul needs
for it to truly soar.

Part Two:
Reaching Out

epiphany

A quiet hush embraced me
in the early morning light;
a pale gold sun reached through
the hues of grey and eggshell blue
to frame my face and sloping hills
of pure-white snow.
Gleaming, twinkling snow
embraced by shades of blue,
crunched beneath my feet,
and softened my voice of defeat.

As a flock of geese soared through the sky,
fading to specks of silver,
I breathed deep and let go of all that made me
bitter.
Puffs of breath escaped in swirls
to dance in the crisp air;
They leapt and joined the atmosphere
returning to be one.

And in that fleeting moment
of nature's grace-filled pause,
an epiphany washed over me -
I no longer felt alone.
Perhaps now it was time
To release resentment,

self-pity,
the wave of regrets.
Perhaps I could honour my pain
by learning to live in the present.

And oh, how precious,
how breathtaking,
the present is -
with golden fields gently dusted in white
and a morning's hopeful sunrise,
reminding me to take life day by day -
to make peace with the unknown -
to feel how the earth supports my feet,
a reminder I am part of a whole:
A single thread in a tapestry,
A jewel in a mosaic,
A paint stroke in God's masterpiece,
A sliver of eternity.

refusing the gaze

This morning when I looked in the mirror
and felt myself recoiling at the reflection –
when the tears began to fall
because my nose is crooked,
my lips too thin,
and my skin is flawed –
I paused and thought to myself:
How many others are doing the same thing right
now?
How many women, young and old,
across this great big globe,
are spending this precious hour peering at their
bodies –
scrutinizing it against a measuring tape –
to see if they meet the gold standard
or if they are just a waste of space?
For is that not what we are told?
We are only worthwhile if we are beautiful?

And yet, between the shame and pain
of believing we need to cover the blemishes
and tuck the rolls away,
something in our soul whispers:
Is this really what my life should be?
Is this body not meant for so much more
than to fade beneath the male gaze?

Is this mind not meant to change the world,
not nitpick all my imperfections?

Imagine all that we could do
if we did not waste our money
on makeup and cheap perfume.
Imagine all the time we'd have
if we stopped criticizing
and engaging in combat
against the very vessel that has kept us alive
all these years:
That has carried us through storms,
up mountains,
through valleys,
and weathered shattering tears.
If we stopped to recognize
the sacredness of our bodies,
the power that they hold,
and the strength that they carry,
we would be an unstoppable force –
our time freed up to change the world.

And maybe that's the reason why
they tell us we don't measure up;
they knew if we ignored
the male fantasy –
they knew if we found our worth
in our own unique shapes –
we would be a force to be reckoned with:

No longer pushed down
by the oppressive burden
and the impossible weight
of a man-made birdcage.

But how does one dismantle
what is hardwired in the brain?
How do we view ourselves with love
instead of the trained disdain?
Empathy,
compassion,
for ourselves
and for each other;
a reminder of what truly matters,
and the souls that soar inside us.

It may not be easy
resisting the well-trodden road,
when choosing to love yourself
pushes against the status quo.
Some days you will still catch yourself
beginning to believe
that the scars or lines define you
and your fragile self-esteem.

It is not your fault you feel this way;
you were taught to feel unworthy
from the first day.
But I hope one day you'll notice

the light in your eyes;
I hope you'll feel a lightness
and free yourself from the confines;
I hope you'll smile at your reflection,
I hope that you'll believe:
You are brilliant and capable
even if you do not fit the definition of "pretty."

omnipresence

It is ok if you cannot find
the love and light you crave
in the building of a church.
It is ok if you are questioning
all the truths that you were fed.
God is not confined to any four walls;
the Divine is not solely hidden
in the ancient words of scripture,
or in any single doctrine in particular.

The Light of this world is already here
in the gentle whispers of the wind,
in the laughter and the joyful tears,
in the stars that dapple like silver jewels
across the satin sky.

The Love of this world is in the very air
you breathe each day of life;
it sustains all of creation
and wraps you in its warmth when you are
with the ones you care for.

The Grace of this world is tugging at your soul;
it invites you to forgive,
to breathe deep.
It reminds that you are welcome here,

and can welcome others in.

The Divine force of the universe
that formed you and me,
nature,
and all the living creatures we see,
is available to you
each and every day.
You do not need church clothes,
cathedral ceilings,
or a rulebook.
The love and light of God is omnipresent;
when you open your eyes,
you will see it.

imprint

How enchanting,
how bewildering,
how beautiful it is
to think that we were chosen
for this small hiccup in the orbit of time;
how each person with whom we cross paths -
even for a moment -
is a miracle,
a gift,
a breath of grace -
an opportunity,
no matter how brief,
to forever alter the course
of each other's lives.
The friend you grew up with,
the clerk at the grocery store,
the family that raised you -
forever leave an imprint on your soul,
and you, on theirs.

<h1 style="text-align:center">gentle release</h1>

Farewell warm affection,
I must let you go;
the road to heartbreak was thrilling
but in the end, it left me cold.

It was sweet but fleeting,
your arms wrapped around mine,
two kisses across my fingertips
and a long, gentle sigh.
What a beautiful, marvelous time it was,
the Earth tilted on its axis,
as we lost ourselves spinning 'round
in a dreamscape of new beginnings.

The spark died,
it is true,
and the colours faded
from vibrant to dull hues.
But I would not wish it away
for any small relief
from the pain of the aftermath
or the inevitable heartache.

The euphoria,
pure joy,
and selfless love you drew from me
have molded me into

the person I am today.
You are forever under my skin -
a part of you always near -
and the memories that we share
will never cease to exist.

And yet,
to reach out and take a step anew,
I must bid you farewell
and return this deep love back to you.
I know my warmth for you will remain,
and your golden glow
will return to visit me
now and then.

I'll still see you in the setting sun,
hear you in a stranger's laugh,
feel you in the whispering breeze
and wish you nothing but the best.
But it's time I find myself again,
remember who I am,
apart from the whole we created
when *we* were all that made sense.

Farewell warm affection:
I send you joy,
I send you peace.
All I ask is that every so often,
you stop and remember me.

extricate

Hush now that critical voice
berating your reflection
and all your hazardous missteps
as you stare into the distance.

You were made for more
than to be held back like a prisoner
by an inner voice of torment
who wants to lock you away forever.

Reality is skewed
by the judge inside your head
who sits looming in a swivel chair
to intimidate and question.

If you listen long enough,
you will merge with the voices
until you cannot find yourself
amidst the scathing, bitter hatred.

Release yourself from false chains –
the handcuffs are a mirage.
you have always been free –
it was your mind that kept you frozen.

Your flaws do not define you;
Your past is not the present;

Your future is not determined;
The possibilities are endless.

ricochet

The darkness that looms
and casts a shadow on one's face
grows larger to cover
the path of another.
The nightmares that keep one awake at night
become another's sleepless plight:
For the pain we inflict,
the injustice we create,
the harsh words we wield,
do not exist in a vacuum.
Suffering ripples throughout generations,
ricochets against the masses,
replicates itself in our DNA,
gets under the skin of our inheritors.
The wheel of brokenness
turns round and round,
and no one is safe
from a definite wound.

And yet, if this is true of the dark,
can it also not be true of the light?
What if the cycle of agony can be broken
by our intentional actions
to make right what was wrong,
to help each other up,
to tear down the walls that keep others out,
to extend the table to all those in need,

to be kind and gracious even to those
not easy to please.
What if the warmth of a fire
can melt the coldest of hearts,
and truth and justice can break
the chains of bondage?
Perhaps sunlight can overcome the shadows
and love can be the ripples
that move through the crowds as
we become who we were meant to.

loyalty

You were there
when you did not understand
what it was to be me –
trapped in a dark tunnel with no end.

When I abandoned you –
left you stranded by the train tracks
as the air turned frigid
and frost crept up the windows –
you did not let it make you bitter.

And when I returned from the battle,
head hung low with no more armour
to cover my open wounds,
you were waiting there patiently
for me to return.

What did I do to deserve
a friendship so strong,
a love so pure,
a loyalty so fierce
that I never gave back to you?

I cannot promise
that history won't repeat;
dark clouds,
they may come
to steal my light again.

But for now,
I'll bring you my summer sun
in the dead of winter;
I'll build a fire to warm
your hands;
I will wake each day
with gratitude
hoping to return the favour.

renewal

I am returning to my soul again:
Cutting away the edges of bitterness hardened
around my heart,
brushing off the dust of disillusion clouding my
vision for too long,
breaking away from chains of fear holding me
back in the dark.
With every new step I take forward,
I break into light,
and find a fresh start.

remember

Remember the way time stopped on that day -
how every problem weighing on your mind
faded into the background
and seemed so insignificant
next to the alarm bells
bellowing the world was coming to an end.

Remember how the ground beneath your feet
shifted -
the hustle and bustle of capitalism drowned out
by the human need for safety,
to be with loved ones
and ensure they were ok.

Remember the perspective gained -
the way the Earth began to heal,
how injustice became obvious,
and we joined to demand equality,
begging for peace to flow like a river.

Remember the way we began to ask ourselves
what do I really need?
When we realized we could do without
half the clothes in our closet -
when we traded in fool's gold
for real, lasting treasure.

Remember how we realized
a slower pace would not kill us,
and perhaps,
might even save us -
when we learned how to embrace the silence and
stillness,
and resist the pressure
of a feverous, soul-crushing busyness.

Capture it like a polaroid;
that moment when we realized
we no longer needed
to prove ourselves -
when we asked:
What path do I want to take in this life
when I ignore the boxed-in walls that abound?

Freeze it in your mind,
how you learned that it was ok
to just be -
to sit in the early morning serenity of a sunrise
and slowly breathe.

Preserve the memory
of light stealing across a frosted windowpane
that holiday in lockdown
when you thought all was lost
but realized one hushed, snow-covered morning
that maybe it was not.

Remember what it taught you.
Resist the temptation
to be coaxed back into the numbing lull
of materialism,
success,
and individualism.

Pandemic or not,
we have a choice in life;
 even without a convenient excuse,
we can choose to take
the road less travelled by.

light within you

On the days when your heart
feels like giving up,
and the weight on your shoulders
is all too much;
In the night, when your thoughts
are much too loud,
and the strength in your bones is giving out:

Take heart,
breathe deep,
you are seen.

When the voices around you scream
"not enough",
and all your plans dissipate
into dust;
When your eyes meet a lonely gaze
in the mirror,
and you wish the reflection would disappear:

Take heart,
breathe deep,
you are loved.

When noise and busy can distract you no more,
and all your hopes lie crushed

on the floor;
When your mind gets to racing,
wondering what's next,
and you can't train your lungs
to take in more breath:

Take heart,
breathe deep,
you are brave.

In the quiet, in the stillness,
in the dark, in the shadows:
Do you not know there's still movement?
Do you not know there's still brilliance?

When your soul is much too tired
and your bones are much too weary,
there is a flame that flickers in you -
a spark of warmth amidst the dreary.

Think of all the flames in each and every chest -
the ones that flicker now
and the ones that came before us -
they've all faced harsh winds,
cold nights,
and black skies;
they've all had moments where they thought
the light would die.

But no matter which way the ground beneath
them shifted,
and even when the time came to leave
earth's existence,
their flames kept on burning in ribbons of gold;
their souls soaring gently to grace the earth
we behold.

So, when you feel there is no reason to stay
and all you once knew is tattered and frayed,
take a step outside late in the night;
tilt your head way up high
towards the twinkling sky.

Take heart,
breathe deep:
You are seen,
You are loved,
You are brave.
You are here to be a part
of this light-filled masterpiece.